HISTORIC CIVILIZATIONS

THE AZTECS

Jeremy Smith
Nicholas Saunders

GARETH **STEVENS**
PUBLISHING
A World Almanac Education Group Company

How to use this book

Each topic in this book is clearly labeled and contains all these components:

Topic heading ———

Introduction to the topic ———

Subtopic 1 gives information about one aspect of the topic. ———

Words that are in the topic glossary are bolded the first time they appear on the page. ———

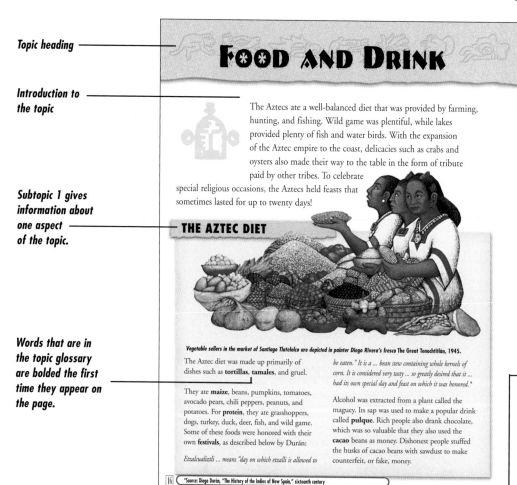

Word Discovery

climate *the ... in an area*
diet *kind of*
divine *rela...*

FOOD AND DRINK

The Aztecs ate a well-balanced diet that was provided by farming, hunting, and fishing. Wild game was plentiful, while lakes provided plenty of fish and water birds. With the expansion of the Aztec empire to the coast, delicacies such as crabs and oysters also made their way to the table in the form of tribute paid by other tribes. To celebrate special religious occasions, the Aztecs held feasts that sometimes lasted for up to twenty days!

THE AZTEC DIET

Vegetable sellers in the market of Santiago Tlatelolco are depicted in painter Diego Rivera's fresco The Great Tenochtitlán, 1945.

The Aztec diet was made up primarily of dishes such as **tortillas**, **tamales**, and gruel.

They ate **maize**, beans, pumpkins, tomatoes, avocado pears, chili peppers, peanuts, and potatoes. For **protein**, they ate grasshoppers, dogs, turkey, duck, deer, fish, and wild game. Some of these foods were honored with their own **festivals**, as described below by Durán:

Etzalcualiztli ... means "day on which etzalli is allowed to

be eaten." It is a ... bean stew containing whole kernels of corn. It is considered very tasty ... so greatly desired that it ... had its own special day and feast on which it was honored.*

Alcohol was extracted from a plant called the maguey. Its sap was used to make a popular drink called **pulque**. Rich people also drank chocolate, which was so valuable that they also used the **cacao** beans as money. Dishonest people stuffed the husks of cacao beans with sawdust to make counterfeit, or fake, money.

Source: Diego Durán, "The History of the Indies of New Spain," sixteenth century

16

AZTEC FARMING

A group of Aztecs are shown constructing chinamp... rafts) in this sixteenth-century painting by Jose M...

As the Aztec population expanded, the task of feeding everybody became more difficult. Farming was hard work, as described below:

The farmer ... is bound to the soil; he works the soil, stirs the soil anew, prepares the soil, he weeds, breaks up the clods, hoes levels the soil, makes furrows ... He removes the undeveloped maize ears, discards the withered ears ... gathers the maize, shucks the ears, removes the ears.

Source: Bernardino de Sahagún, "Florentine Codex," 1580

Glossary

cacao the beans that chocolate and cocoa come from
chinampas gardens grown on artificial islands
comalli Aztec clay cooking griddle (a mesh plate for baking)
festivals days or periods of celebration, often religious
irrigation practice of supplying water by artificial means

See also: Rise of an Empire 6-7, The Aztec Capital 8-9, Grow...

The Glossary explains the meaning of any unusual or difficult words appearing on these two pages.

Please visit our web site at: **www.garethstevens.com**
For a free color catalog describing Gareth Stevens Publishing's list of high-quality books and multimedia programs, call 1-800-542-2595 (USA) or 1-800-387-3178 (Canada). Gareth Stevens Publishing's fax: (414) 332-3567.

Library of Congress Cataloging-in-Publication Data

Smith, Jeremy.
  The Aztecs/ by Jeremy Smith and Nicholas Saunders.
    p. cm. — (Historic civilizations)
  Includes index.
  ISBN 0-8368-4201-4 (lib. bdg.)
  1. Aztecs—History. 2. Aztecs—Social life and customs. I. Saunders, Nicholas.
II. Title. III. Series.
F1219.73.S575 2004
972—dc22

2004045326

This North American edition first published in 2005 by
Gareth Stevens Publishing
A World Almanac Education Group Company
330 West Olive Street, Suite 100
Milwaukee, Wisconsin 53212 USA

This U.S. edition copyright © 2005 by Gareth Stevens, Inc. Original edition copyright © 2004 ticktock Entertainment Ltd. First published in Great Britain in 2004 as *Your Aztec Homework Helper* by ticktock Media Ltd., Unit 2, Orchard Business Centre, North Farm Road, Tunbridge Wells, Kent TN23XF, UK.

The publishers wish to thank Egan-Reid Ltd. for their research and consulting expertise in the making of this book.

Gareth Stevens editor: Barbara Kiely Miller
Gareth Stevens cover design: Steve Schraenkler

Printed in the United States of America

1 2 3 4 5 6 7 8 9 08 07 06 05 04

2

Contents

Subtopic 2 gives information about another aspect of the topic.

Discover other words that relate to the topic.

The Case Study is a closer look at a famous person, artifact, or building that relates to the topic.

Each photo or illustration is described and discussed in the accompanying text.

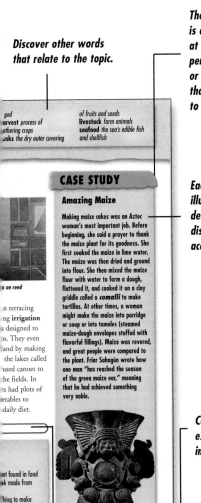

god
harvest *process of gathering crops*
husks *the dry outer covering*

of fruits and seeds
livestock *farm animals*
seafood *the sea's edible fish and shellfish*

...s on reed

...n terracing
...ng **irrigation**
... designed to
...s. They even
...and by making
... the lakes called
...used canoes to
...he fields. In
...s had plots of
...etables to
...daily diet.

CASE STUDY

Amazing Maize

Making maize cakes was an Aztec woman's most important job. Before beginning, she said a prayer to thank the maize plant for its goodness. She first soaked the maize in lime water. The maize was then dried and ground into flour. She then mixed the maize flour with water to form a dough, flattened it, and cooked it on a clay griddle called a *comalli* to make tortillas. At other times, a woman might make the maize into porridge or soup or into tamales (steamed maize-dough envelopes stuffed with flavorful fillings). Maize was revered, and great people were compared to the plant. Friar Sahagún wrote how one man "has reached the season of the green maize ear," meaning that he had achieved something very noble.

...nt found in food
...k made from

...hing to make

...ith a meat filling
...ed bread

Xilonen, goddess of maize, on an Aztec polychrome brazier (pan to hold burning coals) from Tlatelolco, Mexico

*Source: Bernardino de Sahagún, "Florentine Codex," 1580

Captions clearly explain what is in the picture.

At the bottom of some sections, a reference bar tells where the information has come from.

Other pages in the book that relate to what you have read in this topic are listed here.

A reference bar marked with an asterisk (*) gives the source of the quotations in the text.

✴ORIGIN ✴OF ✴THE ✴AZTECS

The most famous **civilization** to ever live in the volcanic highlands of central Mexico is probably that of the Aztecs. In 1325, they arrived on the shores of Lake Texcoco, where they built their capital Tenochtitlán. The Aztecs developed a powerful empire that spread across Central America, yet it existed for barely three centuries before being destroyed in 1521 by Spaniard Hernán Cortés and his troops.

A NOMADIC TRIBE

The group of people known as the **Mexica**, or *Aztecs*, was based in northern Mexico during the early part of their history.

Friar Diego Durán was a Spaniard who grew up in Mexico City in the sixteenth century and who learned about the Aztecs by interviewing the natives. According to Durán, the Aztecs got their name from the place where they had once lived:

The land they inhabited ... was called Aztlán, which means Whiteness or the Place of Herons, and this is why these nations were called Aztec, which signifies "The People of Whiteness."*

Between 1100 and 1200, the Aztecs left their home in search of more land. In about 1300, they arrived in the Valley of Mexico at the city of Culhuacán. They persuaded the local Culhua king to let them settle there, but in 1323, they were driven out of the city. Some

This depiction of the Aztecs' long **migration** before founding the city of Tenochtitlán comes from the Codex Boturini.

accounts say that they were forced to leave because the Aztecs had **sacrificed** the king's favorite daughter after being told to do so by the god **Huitzilopochtli**.

*Source: Diego Durán, "The History of the Indies of New Spain," 1581

Word Discovery

culture *arts, customs, and beliefs of a people*
independent nation *a country*

that rules itself
origin *beginning of something*
prophesy *mystic or divine*

prediction
settlement *place where people set up a community*

VALLEY OF MEXICO

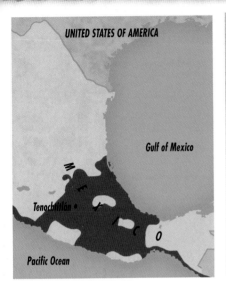

= Volcano

Maps of the Valley of Mexico (right) and the territory of the Aztec Empire (left) are shown above. The yellow areas span the length of present-day Mexico, while the red areas show the extent of the Aztec Empire in 1519.

The Valley of Mexico is a large valley surrounded by volcanoes. Lake Texcoco sits in the center of the valley. The Mexica built their capital city on an island in the middle of this salty lake. The valley has rich soil and receives a lot of rain during spring, although for most of the year the land is dry and brown. About one million Aztecs made their home in the Valley of Mexico, while the highland valleys and plains that surrounded it provided a home for over two million more Aztecs.

Glossary

civilization a culture and its people
Huitzilopochtli the Aztec god of war and the sun and the Aztecs' guardian god
legend a story from the past which is believed to be true but which cannot be proven
Mexica the powerful **tribe** that founded Tenochtitlán
migration moving from one area to another
sacrificed killed as an offering to a god
tribe group of people who have a common culture and who think of themselves as one

CASE STUDY

Finding a Home

In 1325, the Aztecs settled and began to build a city at a place they named *Tenochtitlán* or "Place of the Prickly Pear Cactus." The city's location, which Aztec legend says was foretold, was on an island in the middle of Lake Texcoco. The god Huitzilopochtli had appeared in a vision to an Aztec priest and told him to look for an eagle with a serpent in its beak and sitting on a cactus on an island in the middle of the lake. Native manuscripts state that this divine instruction came true:

And when the eagle saw the Mexicans, he bowed his head low ... And the god called out to them, he said to them, "O Mexicans, it shall be there!" And then the Mexicans wept, they said, "O happy, O blessed are we! We have beheld the city that shall be ours."*

In this illustration from the Florentine Codex, migration leaders are shown spotting the eagle with a serpent in its beak.

*Source: Fernando Alvarado Tezozomoc, "Cronica Mexicayotl," 1609

See also: Rise of an Empire 6-7, Aztec Time 20-21, Religion and Sacrifice 24-25, The End of the Aztecs 30-32

5

RISE OF AN EMPIRE

When the Aztecs first arrived in the Valley of Mexico, they found that they were not the most powerful people living there. Two tribes — the Tepanecs and Acolhua — dwarfed the Aztecs in terms of size, influence, and advances. To establish themselves in the area, the Aztecs allied themselves with the Tepanecs and helped them build an **empire**. As the Aztecs themselves became stronger, however, they wanted their own king. In 1372, they appointed a local nobleman named Acamapichtli to be their ***tlatoani***, or king, and at the beginning of the fifteenth century, led by King Itzcoatl, the Aztecs rose up against their rulers and overthrew them.

THE TRIPLE ALLIANCE

By 1426, hostilities were growing between the Aztecs and their allies the Tepanecs. War erupted, and in 1428 an **alliance** between the people of Tenochtitlán and the nearby settlements of Huexotzinco, Texcoco, and Tlacopán defeated the powerful Tepanecs, who lived west of Tenochtitlán. The Huexotzinca returned to their **traditional** home, but the other three groups drew up an agreement not to attack each other and to band together to conquer other towns. The *Codex Chimalpopoca* describes the victory of the Aztecs:

In that year 1432, the Tenochtitlán ruler Itzcoatzin (Itzcoatl) was able to come out into the open, for he ruled everywhere, over rulers from town to town. *

The fighting at Tlatelolco in Texcoco is shown in the manuscript The Theatre in New Spain, by Panos, c. eighteenth century.

*Source: "Codex Chimalpopoca," sixteenth century

Word Discovery

censor *to block or delete something that is objectionable*
civilized *having a high level of cultural development*

conquest *taking over something, often by force*
lineage *line of descent from common ancestors*

usurp *to take by force*
wealth *a great sum of money or material possessions*

REWRITING HISTORY

Before the Aztecs, a people called the Toltecs ruled over highland central Mexico. In about 1170, the Toltec culture collapsed and the Chichimec (a name meaning "peoples of the lineage of the dog," or uncivilized people) from the north invaded Mexico. Aztec king Itzcoatl wanted to make sure that his people would not be linked to the lowly Chichimec, so he ordered the existing history books burned and had scribes write a new history. This version said that the Mexica were the special people of the god Huitzilopochtli and that their rulers were descended from the civilized Toltec kings:

It is not wise that all the people should know the paintings. The common people would be driven to ruin and there would be trouble, because these paintings contain many lies. For many in the pictures have been hailed as gods. *

This stone statue of a warrior is from the Toltec city of Tula.

*Source: Bernardino de Sahagún, "Códice Matritense de la Real Academia", sixteenth century

CASE STUDY

Tribute from sixteen towns, including women's tunics and skirts and warrior costumes and shields, is recorded in this excerpt from the Codex Mendoza, p robably written in the early 1540s.

Paying Tribute

As the fifteenth century progressed, the Aztec empire continued to grow. When the Aztecs captured a new territory, the conquered people were usually allowed to rule themselves but were made to pay an annual tax called a **tribute** to the Aztec emperor. As a result, a staggering amount of riches flowed into the capital city of Tenochtitlán. In his account of the Aztecs, Friar Diego Durán describes the types of goods that the people of the empire had to pay:

The subjects of the lords of Tenochtitlán paid all kinds of tribute — food, clothing, weapons ... The poorest among them, lacking what was necessary, offered their sons and daughters. *

*Source: Diego Durán, "The History of the Indies of New Spain," 1581

Glossary

alliance a union formed between two or more parties to pursue common interests for their mutual benefit
empire a group of lands controlled by a single ruler or country
tlatoani a king or emperor of the Mexica tribe and, later, of the Aztecs

traditional established or customary as a place or way of doing something
tribute payment made by conquered people to another, more powerful nation

See also: Origin of the Aztecs 4-5, The Aztec Capital 8-9, Language and Writing 10-11, Aztec Rulers 14-15

THE AZTEC CAPITAL

The Aztec capital of Tenochtitlán now lies underneath the streets of present-day Mexico City. Today, bits of the Aztec city often emerge when building construction takes place in the Mexican capital. Temples, sacrificial platforms, and statues of gods have all been discovered in recent years. At its height, Tenochtitlán would have been a vibrant and bustling place, dominated by the Great Temple and the market at Tlatelolco, just outside the city.

THE FOUNDING OF TENOCHTITLÁN

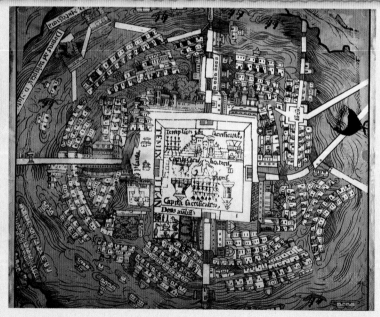

Despite the fact that the site chosen for Tenochtitlán was **swampland**, the Aztec builders conquered the difficult terrain.

Friar Diego Durán recorded the way in which this was done after interviewing area natives:

This map of Tenochtitlán is believed to have been made by Hernán Cortés.

Little by little they ... created space for their city; on top of the water they made a foundation with earth and stones that were thrown into the spaces between the stakes, in order to lay out their city on that surface. *

The *Codex Mendoza*'s opening page shows that the city was divided into four **quarters**. By measuring the **orientation** of buildings and examining sixteenth-century Spanish maps, archaeologists have shown that Tenochtitlán was built on a **grid plan** aligned with the gods. The east-west line was considered the most important because it tracked the path of the sun god Tonatiuh across the sky.

*Source: Diego Durán, "The History of the Indies of New Spain," 1581

Word Discovery

astound *surprise or shock*
barter *exchange goods for other goods or services*

construct *build something*
dense *close together*
magnitude *of great size or importance*

sprawling *something that spreads over a large area*

SPANISH IMPRESSIONS

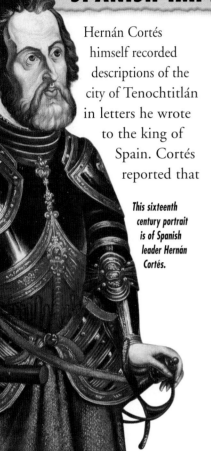

This sixteenth century portrait is of Spanish leader Hernán Cortés.

Hernán Cortés himself recorded descriptions of the city of Tenochtitlán in letters he wrote to the king of Spain. Cortés reported that it had sixty thousand houses and covered an area of 5 square miles (13 square kilometers):

The city is so big and so remarkable ... with as good buildings and many more people than Granada had when it was taken. *(1)

Spanish foot soldier Bernal Díaz del Castillo was also stunned by the **scale** of the city:

*... when we saw all those cities and villages built in the water, and that straight and level **causeway** leading to the city, we were astounded. It all seemed so like a **vision** from a fantasy story that some of our soldiers asked if it was a dream. It was so wonderful that I do not know how to describe the first sight of things never seen, or heard of, or dreamed of before.* *(2)

*Source: (1) Hernán Cortés, Letters from Mexico, sixteenth century; (2) Bernal Díaz del Castillo, "The Conquest of New Spain," sixteenth century

CASE STUDY

D. Hernandez Xochitiotzin's mural, Market in Tlaxcala, shows daily life before the Spanish conquest.

The Great Market

Aztecs flocked to a great market at Tlatelolco, just outside Tenochtitlán. Spanish priest Bernardino de Sahagún reported that up to sixty thousand people went to market every day, and that "given the choice between going to market and going to heaven, the normal Aztec housewife chose heaven, but asked if she could go to the market first!" His writings in the *Florentine Codex* also give a glimpse of how traders bought and sold:

The ruler took care of the directing of the marketplace and all things sold, for the good of the common folk ... so that these might not be abused, not suffer harm, not be deceived, not disdained .... Marketplace directors were appointed to office. Each of the directors took care, and was charged, that no one might deceive another, and how (articles) might be priced and sold.

Glossary

causeway a raised road built to get across water
grid plan roads laid out in evenly spaced, horizontal and vertical lines at right angles to each other
orientation position and direction
quarters main divisions or areas of a city (sometimes a city has more than four quarters)
scale size or extent
swampland area of waterlogged ground that may be partially underwater
vision something seen in a dream

See also: Origin of the Aztecs 4-5, Rise of an Empire 6-7, Homes 12-13, The End of the Aztecs 30-31

*Source: Bernardino de Sahagún, "Florentine Codex"

LANGUAGE AND WRITING

The Aztecs recorded their history using a picture-based language called *pictographs*. **Scribes** drew the pictographs in special books called **codices**. When the Spanish took control of Mexico in 1519, the new Christian rulers burned any books they could find, viewing them as unholy. Only one pre-conquest example of Aztec writing survives. Other examples of the Aztec language that exist today are codices drawn after the Spanish conquest.

AZTEC CODICES

The Aztecs used pictures, or **glyphs**, for their writing system, just as the Chinese and Japanese have.

Some glyphs were drawings of objects, and others were meant to show ideas. For example, a picture of a shield and a club meant war. Aztec glyphs were carved on objects, such as stone monuments and tiny jade beads, painted on walls and vases, and painted in books made of bark called codices. Many glyphs were calendar and numeric signs, but some represented historic events. These can be seen in the *Codex Mendoza*, which documents the Aztec army's conquest of other cities. To show that a city has been conquered, the city's name is written next to the "conquered" glyph, which shows a temple, or pyramid, sending out smoke and flames and with its top falling over.

These illustrations from the Codex Mendoza show the "burning-temple" glyph, which represents a conquered city.

Word Discovery

account *story of an event*
bias *distortion of the facts based on one's personal feelings*

dialect *a variety of a language used by people in one region*
ritual *the words or acts*

performed in a ceremony
traditional *done according to local custom*

WRITTEN RECORDS

Aztec books had no covers but were protected by a wooden board at each end when they were folded up.

Running the Aztec empire meant that scribes were busy people. Some recorded who had paid taxes, some kept records of accounts, and others were in charge of temple libraries. One Aztec ruler describes just how many scribes there were in Aztec society:

*They had scribes for each branch of knowledge. Some dealt with the **annals**, putting down in order the things which happened each year, giving the day,*

*month, and hour. Others ... recorded the lineage of rulers, lords, and noblemen, registering the newborn and deleting those who had died. The priests recorded all matters to do with the temples and images ... and finally, the philosophers and learned men which there were among them were charged with painting all the sciences which they had discovered, and with teaching by memory all the songs in which were **embodied** their scientific knowledge and historical traditions.**

*Source: Fernando de Avala Ixtlilxochitl, "Historia Tolteca-Chichimeca," c. 1550

Glossary

annals yearly historical records
codices (singular: codex) books made by folding pages
embodied included as part of
glyphs picture symbols for words,

phrases, or sounds
Nahuatl the Aztec language
scribes professional writers
source document or person providing information about a topic

CASE STUDY

The Florentine Codex and the Codex Mendoza

The *Florentine Codex* was compiled by Friar Bernardino de Sahagún between 1577 and 1580. He spoke to old Aztec survivors and asked them to paint their stories in the traditional Mexica way. The native text, *Nahuatl,* appears in the right column of the book, with Spanish text in the left column. This codex provides a rich **source** of information about the Aztec view of life. It gives details about their health, lifestyles, rituals, attitudes towards law and order, drunkenness, and even Aztec jokes!

The *Codex Mendoza* was prepared for King Charles V of Spain. It was written using the native pictographic system of writing. Explanations of what the glyphs mean were written in the margins by a Spanish priest. It gives facts about customs, rites, everyday life, and some of the many signs, or glyphs, such as those used to represent place names and titles of warriors.

Illustration from Codex Mendoza showing tribute list paid by a city, including precious greenstones and clothing.

See also: The Aztec Capital 8–9, Growing Up Aztec 18–19, Aztec Society 22–23, The End of the Aztecs 30–31

Source: Ixtlilxochitl, "Historia Tolteca-Chichimeca"

HOMES

Remains of Aztec buildings and paintings in the codices provide a wealth of information about how the Aztecs lived. Nobles resided in big houses with flat roofs and two stories. Peasants lived in houses that were much smaller and often built in groups. When the Spanish arrived, they were impressed with the skill with which the Aztecs built their homes. Soldier Bernal Díaz del Castillo, who traveled to Mexico with Cortés' army, observed that his lodging had been prepared with such skill "that one of the horsemen took the shining whiteness for silver and came galloping back to tell Cortés that our quarters had silver walls."

RICH AND POOR

Archaeologists have discovered the remains of houses once occupied by Aztec peasants. These ruins show that, although some houses had stone walls, most had **mud-brick** walls and thatched roofs made from **maguey** leaves.

Peasant houses are often found in a group, called a **cemithualtin**, of five or six buildings clustered around a courtyard. These houses are often so tiny that everything — cooking, washing, working, and relaxing — must have taken place outside in the courtyard.

Wealthy citizens lived in bigger houses that were hidden behind windowless walls. Inside, rooms opened onto a central courtyard that often had a pond and gardens of brightly colored flowers. In all houses, however, everybody slept on mats, as noted by Bernal Díaz del Castillo:

*However great a lord he might be, no one had any bed other than this kind.**

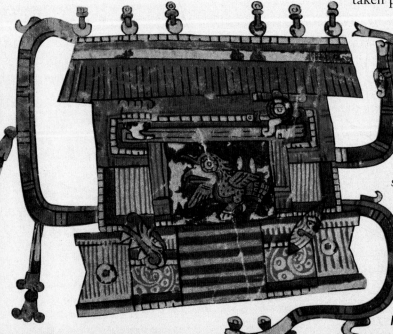

The House of Rain— an example of a fine Aztec house from the Codex Vaticanus, sixteenth century

*Source: Bernal Diaz del Castillo, "The Conquest of New Spain", sixteenth century

HOUSING

Ruins at the villages of Capilco and Cuexcomate show what life might have been like in the Aztec countryside. The small farming hamlet of Capilco had twenty-one houses, while Cuexcomate had one-hundred-fifty. Houses were tiny, and most activity probably took place outside on the patio. Archaeologists have found hundreds of **artifacts** alongside these houses, suggesting that garbage was tossed there by the inhabitants. Friar Sahagún recorded a similar finding:

*Aztec babies spend their time piling up earth and **potsherds**, those on the ground.* *

These ruins are of the Aztec settlement at Cuexcomate.

In the later Aztec period, it appears that the population was growing. Excavations have uncovered evidence of increased dam building, which would have been needed to irrigate more land and produce more food.

*Source: Friar Bernardino de Sahagún, "Florentine Codex: General History of the Things of New Spain, " sixteenth century

Glossary

artifacts cultural objects from the past

cemithualtin a Nahuatl word meaning a group of peasant houses

mud-brick rectangular brick made from dried mud and straw

maguey a plant used for brewing alcohol, making roofs, and plaiting into threads

potsherds pieces of broken pottery

CASE STUDY

This photograph captures part of the ruined palace at Yautepec, Mexico.

An Aztec Palace

In 1989, in the modern town of Yautepec, Mexico, archaeologists discovered an enormous stone platform covering more than an acre (half a hectare). It had been the site of the palace of the powerful tlatoani, or rulers, of Yautepec. The archaeologists discovered that the walls of the stone palace had been 13 feet (4 meters) high and that the only entrance was at the top of a single stairway. The platform held many courtyards, rooms, and passages, all constructed of stone covered with layers of lime plaster and decorated with colorful paintings. This was the first Aztec royal palace to be excavated. A plain stone wall outside kept out the public. Inside, the buildings faced a central courtyard.

RULERS

In 1372, Acamapichtli became the first Aztec *tlatoani*, meaning emperor or king. He was succeeded by Huitzilihuitl, under whom the city of Tenochtitlán continued to grow. Led by their fourth emperor, Itzcoatl, the Aztecs defeated their neighbors and established a powerful empire, laying the foundations upon which future emperors would build.

AZTEC RULERS

Acamapichtli (1372–1391)
Huitzilihuitl (1391–1415)
Chimalpopoca (1415–1426)
Itzcoatl (1426–1440)
Moctezuma I (1440-1468)
Axayacatl (1468–1481)
Tizoc (1481–1486)
Ahuitzotl (1486–1502)
Moctezuma II (1502–1520)
Cuitlahuac (1520)
Cuauhtemoc (1520–1525)

MOCTEZUMA I

Emperor Moctezuma I **succeeded** Itzcoatl in 1440. Building upon the success of his **predecessor**, Moctezuma expanded the Aztec empire even further.

He added new territory by invading tropical areas of Mexico, including the city of Coixtlahuaca in 1458. Moctezuma also introduced a number of **reforms** that changed Aztec society. Spanish friar Diego Durán wrote about Moctezuma's introduction of a series of new laws that served to further widen the distinction between nobles and **commoners**:

- *Only the king and the prime minister ... may wear sandals within the palace.*
- *The commoners will not be allowed to wear cotton clothing, under pain of death, but can only use garments of maguey fiber.*
- *Only the great noblemen and valiant warriors are given license to build a house with a second story; for disobeying this law a person receives the death penalty.*
- *Thieves will be sold for the price of their theft, unless the theft be grave, having been committed many times. Such thieves will be punished by death.**

Moctezuma did allow some commoners to gain influence through their own talents. He created a new position called *Quauhpilli* — Eagle Lord. This rank was awarded to the bravest soldiers in his army.

This image of Moctezuma I comes from the Codex Mendoza.

*Source: Diego Durán, "The History of the Indies of New Spain," sixteenth century

Word Discovery

autocrat *ruler with total power*
coronation *ceremony of crowning a king, queen, or emperor*

imperial *related to an empire or emperor*
legislation *laws*

slaughter *killing a large number of people; killing livestock*
society *people living together in a community*

MOCTEZUMA II

Beginning in the 1470s, the Aztec Empire suffered a series of setbacks, including the 1486 murder of Emperor Tizoc. His brother Ahuitzotl ruled for the next sixteen years before Moctezuma II came to power in 1502. As the new emperor, Moctezuma II removed many officials who had served under Ahuitzotl. The empire swelled under its new leader, but it failed to defeat the Tlaxcala, its powerful neighbors. Moctezuma was fearful about the future, and Nezahualpilli, a former king of Texcoco, appeared to him in a dream. In the words of Diego Durán:

Nezahualpilli spoke to Moctezuma in a dream as follows, showing him the future portents. "I must inform you of strange and marvelous things which must come about during your reign."*

Moctezuma II, who lived from 1466–1520, in a sixteenth-century image.

*Source: Diego Durán, "The History of the Indies of New Spain," sixteenth century

Glossary

commoners ordinary people, not of the noble class
predecessor person who held a job before the current person in that position
Quauhpilli a Nahuatl word meaning Eagle lords. Until the reign of Moctezuma II, successful warriors could rise in rank to become nobles.
reforms improvements or changes
seclusion being alone
succeeded came after another in a job
Tezcatlipoca the Aztec god of night and material things

CASE STUDY

The coronation of Moctezuma II, as shown in the Historia de los Indios *by Diego Durán, 1579.*

The Power of the Emperor

Diego Durán's *Historia de los Indios* tells archaeologists about the power that an emperor had in Aztec society. It shows rulers seated on thrones covered with the skins of powerful animals, such as jaguars. This codex also records the coronation of emperors during which they prayed to their patron god **Tezcatlipoca** for guidance and identified themselves with him. Spanish priest Sahagún also shows the final ceremony of the imperial coronation involving a period of **seclusion** and blood offerings.

See also: Rise of an Empire 6-7, Homes 12-13, Wars and Weapons 26-27, The End of the Aztecs 30-31

FOOD AND DRINK

The Aztecs ate a well-balanced diet that was provided by farming, hunting, and fishing. Wild game was plentiful, while lakes provided plenty of fish and water birds. With the expansion of the Aztec empire to the coast, delicacies such as crabs and oysters also made their way to the table in the form of tribute paid by other tribes. To celebrate special religious occasions, the Aztecs held feasts that sometimes lasted for up to twenty days!

THE AZTEC DIET

Vegetable sellers in the market of Santiago Tlatelolco are depicted in painter Diego Rivera's fresco The Great Tenochtitlán, 1945.

The Aztec diet was made up primarily of dishes such as **tortillas**, **tamales**, and gruel.

They ate **maize**, beans, pumpkins, tomatoes, avocado pears, chili peppers, peanuts, and potatoes. For **protein**, they ate grasshoppers, dogs, turkey, duck, deer, fish, and wild game. Some of these foods were honored with their own **festivals**, as described below by Durán:

Etzalcualiztli ... means "day on which etzalli is allowed to be eaten." It is a ... bean stew containing whole kernels of corn. It is considered very tasty ... so greatly desired that it ... had its own special day and feast on which it was honored.*

Alcohol was extracted from a plant called the maguey. Its sap was used to make a popular drink called **pulque**. Rich people also drank chocolate, which was so valuable that they also used the **cacao** beans as money. Dishonest people stuffed the husks of cacao beans with sawdust to make counterfeit, or fake, money.

*Source: Diego Durán, "The History of the Indies of New Spain," sixteenth century

Word Discovery

climate the weather conditions in an area
diet kind of food a person eats
divine related to or coming from a god
harvest process of gathering crops
husks the dry outer covering of fruits and seeds
livestock farm animals
seafood the sea's edible fish and shellfish

AZTEC FARMING

A group of Aztecs are shown constructing chinampas (small floating gardens on reed rafts) in this sixteenth-century painting by Jose Muro Pico.

As the Aztec population expanded, the task of feeding everybody became more difficult. Farming was hard work, as described below:

The farmer ... is bound to the soil; he works the soil, stirs the soil anew, prepares the soil, he weeds, breaks up the clods, hoes levels the soil, makes furrows ... He removes the undeveloped maize ears, discards the withered ears ... gathers the maize, shucks the ears, removes the ears.*

Aztec farmers began terracing farm fields and using **irrigation** and other methods designed to produce more crops. They even farmed on swampland by making artificial islands in the lakes called *chinampas*. They used canoes to navigate between the fields. In town, most families had plots of land and grew vegetables to **supplement** their daily diet.

*Source: Bernardino de Sahagún, "Florentine Codex," 1580

Glossary

cacao the beans that chocolate and cocoa come from
chinampas gardens grown on artificial islands
comalli Aztec clay cooking griddle (a mesh plate for baking)
festivals days or periods of celebration, often religious
irrigation practice of supplying water by artificial means

maize a type of corn
protein essential element found in food
pulque an alcoholic drink made from maguey sap
supplement add something to make up for deficiencies
tamales maize husks with a meat filling
tortillas thin, unleavened bread

See also: Rise of an Empire 6-7, The Aztec Capital 8-9, Growing Up Aztec 18-19

CASE STUDY

Amazing Maize

Making maize cakes was an Aztec woman's most important job. Before beginning, she said a prayer to thank the maize plant for its goodness. She first soaked the maize in lime water. The maize was then dried and ground into flour. She then mixed the maize flour with water to form a dough, flattened it, and cooked it on a clay griddle called a *comalli* to make tortillas. At other times, a woman might make the maize into porridge or soup or into tamales (steamed maize-dough envelopes stuffed with flavorful fillings). Maize was revered, and great people were compared to the plant. Friar Sahagún wrote how one man "has reached the season of the green maize ear," meaning that he had achieved something very noble.

Xilonen, goddess of maize, on an Aztec polychrome brazier (pan to hold burning coals) from Tlatelolco, Mexico

*Source: Bernardino de Sahagún, "Florentine Codex," 1580

GROWING UP AZTEC

Aztec boys began attending school at age fifteen. Commoners went to schools called *telpochcalli*. Students learned manual skills and how to sing and dance. They also received **military** training from experienced warriors. Noble children went to more exclusive schools known as *calmecac*. Associated with temples, the aim of the calmecac was to educate the next generation of leaders in government, the priesthood, and the army. The calmecac were well stocked with codices that students used to learn about the gods, warfare, and **astronomical** events.

EDUCATION

These pages from the *Codex Mendoza* reveal much about the future of Aztec children.

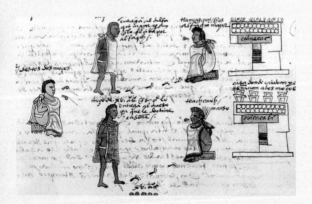

BOYS

There were two paths of further education for boys to take. A father (*pictured on the left above*) could send his son to the head priest (*top*) for training at the temple school, or calmecac, for noble boys. Alternatively (*below*), he could turn his son over to the master of youths at the "young men's house," or telpochcalli, where a military training was provided for commoners.

GIRLS

When a girl turned fifteen, she was ready to get married. At the bottom of this picture (*below*), a torch-lit procession is shown accompanying the bride to the groom's house on the first night. A feast is laid out inside. Four older wedding guests are shown talking. The bride and her older groom, their garments tied together, sit, in front of a hearth and a bowl of incense, on the mat on which they will eventually sleep.

Source: "Codex Mendoza," fourteenth century

Word Discovery

breadwinner *person who earns money to support a family*
instruction *teaching*

matchmaker *person who arranges marriages for others*
nurture *develop and nourish*

occupation *job or profession*
upbringing *the way that parents raise their children*

MARRIED LIFE

A miniature mask represented the god Ixtiton, who brought children a peaceful sleep.

Right after they were married, Aztec couples tried to have children. Babies were delivered by professional **midwives** who cut the umbilical cord and prayed to Chalchiuhtlicue, the goddess of fertility. Soon after birth, baby boys were given miniature **symbols** of their future adult life based upon their father's occupation, such as a warrior's shield. Baby girls were given a broom, a spindle full of cotton thread, or a basket. Children were also given masks, like the one on the left, to help them sleep peacefully. Once married, the husband might be away from home for much of the year, often fighting for the emperor, and the wife was left behind to take care of the household. A man's role was to protect his wife and earn enough money to support the family. A woman was expected to be obedient to her husband. The *Codex Nuttall* reveals that wives were told:

*Obey your husband cheerfully. Do not scorn him for you will offend the goddess **Xochiquetzal**.* *

*Source: "Codex Nuttall," sixteenth century

Glossary

astronomical related to the study of the stars, planets, and outer space
midwives people trained to assist women with childbirth
military related to soldiers, weapons, or war

symbols objects that represent something else
Xochiquetzal goddess of beauty, love, and housekeeping

CASE STUDY

Stone workers are shown hewing and crafting stone in this image from the Florentine Codex, c.1570

Duties of Man

Indian poems reveal the Aztecs' expectations of a man's life:

Act! Cut wood, work the land, plant cactus, sow maguey; you shall have drink, food, clothing. With this you will stand straight, With this you shall live. For this you shall be spoken of, praised; in this manner you will show yourself to your parents and relatives. Someday you shall tie yourself to a skirt and blouse. What will she drink? What will she eat? You are the support, the remedy; you are the eagle, the tiger. Do not throw yourself upon women ... Hold back with your heart until you are a grown man, strong and robust. *

*Source: Miguel León-Portilla, "Aztec Thought and Culture," sixteenth century

See also: Language and Writing 10-11, Food and Drink 16-17, Aztec Society 22-23, Wars and Weapons 26-27

AZTEC TIME

The Aztecs believed that four worlds had existed before this one and that all four had been destroyed. They believed that they were living in the "fifth sun" under the sun god Tonatiuh. They also believed that at any time the world they lived in could be destroyed by fiery rain and that they would all be turned into dogs, turkeys, and butterflies. The Aztecs used two calendars — a **solar** calendar that lasted 365 days and a religious calendar that lasted 260 days, known as the ***tonalpohualli***. Their use of both calendars together meant that the same calendar date reoccurred only once every fifty-two years.

THE STONE OF THE SUN

The Stone of the Sun is a large circular stone slab that was found in Tenochtitlán in 1760. It is carved with intricate designs that would have once been vibrantly colored, as shown in this reproduction. The stone shows the five periods, or "suns," of creation in Aztec mythology. The Stone of the Sun gives us the Aztecs' history of their universe.

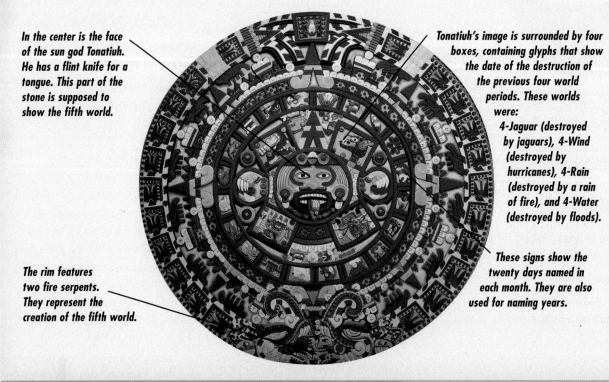

In the center is the face of the sun god Tonatiuh. He has a flint knife for a tongue. This part of the stone is supposed to show the fifth world.

Tonatiuh's image is surrounded by four boxes, containing glyphs that show the date of the destruction of the previous four world periods. These worlds were: 4-Jaguar (destroyed by jaguars), 4-Wind (destroyed by hurricanes), 4-Rain (destroyed by a rain of fire), and 4-Water (destroyed by floods).

These signs show the twenty days named in each month. They are also used for naming years.

The rim features two fire serpents. They represent the creation of the fifth world.

Source: Museum of Archaeology and History, Mexico; stone creation in late fifteenth century

Word Discovery

destruction *damage that is so severe that the item broken cannot be repaired or saved*

doom *certain destruction*
fate *development of events that cannot be controlled*

prediction *a guess that an event will happen in the future*
rebirth *a new or second start*

THE RELIGIOUS CALENDAR

This image from the Codex Borbonicus shows the male and female gods of creation discussing the organization of time. The male god Ometecuhtli is on the right, and the female god Omecihuatl is on the left.

Priests kept notes of the 260-day religious calendar, tonalpohualli, in sacred books known as *tonalamatl*. The most famous example of a tonalamatl is the *Codex Borbonicus*. The pages of this codex show the thirteen lords of the day and nine lords of the night. Their images were arranged to show their power over individual hours and days and also over important thirteen-day weeks. Tonalamatl were thought to have magical properties and were used by priests to make predictions.

Glossary

extinguished stopped the burning of something; brought to an end
sacrificed killed as an offering to a god; other valuable items may also be given or offered up

solar related to the Sun
tonalpohualli the Aztec religious calendar based on twenty weeks of thirteen days each

CASE STUDY

The New Fire Ceremony

When a cycle of fifty-two years neared its end, the Aztecs believed that the future of the world was uncertain. Five days before the end of the cycle, they **extinguished** all fires, threw away all of their belongings, and cleaned their homes in preparation for the end of the world. On the night before the end of the cycle, priests marched to the Hill of the Star outside Tenochtitlán. A human victim was **sacrificed** by lighting a fire in his chest and burning his heart. Runners lit torches from the fire and took the flames to their own communities. The next day, people put on new clothes, bought new things for their homes, and whitewashed their houses. Humankind was saved!

This scene from the Codex Borbonicus shows the New Fire Ceremony.

See also: Language and Writing 10-11, Religion and Sacrifice 24-25, The End of the Aztecs 30-31

AZTEC SOCIETY

Aztec **society** and behavior were very regimented. The emperor was at the top of society, with nobles, or *pipiltin*, ranked below him. Beneath the nobles were the commoners, or *macehualtin*, and at the bottom of Aztec society were the slaves. People had to follow strict **social codes**, with fierce punishments for anyone who broke them. Thieves were sold as slaves or put to death.

NOBLES AND COMMONERS

Nobles ran the religious, **economic**, and political systems of daily life.

Nobles did not have to pay any taxes and were provided with an official residence from whose farm lands they made their **livelihood**. The emperor, or tlatoani, controlled all the nobles, although it was possible for a nobleman to rise to the position of emperor. Historian Alonso de Zorita recorded the way in which this could happen:

*When there were no brothers to choose from ... the council elected the most capable relative of the deceased ruler; and if there was none, they chose another noble, but they never elected a ... common man.**

Commoners, or the *macehualtin*, were organized into hereditary **clans** known as *calpulli* that were further divided into units of twenty families and arranged in groups of one hundred households. Each calpulli had its own school and temple and was controlled by a leader who was elected for life. The benefits of belonging to a calpulli were not given to the free but landless peasants known as *mayeques*.

The Codex Mendoza depicts Aztec nobles wearing their distinctive cloaks and jewelry and seated on reed thrones.

*Source: Alonso de Zorita, sixteenth century

Word Discovery

behavior *the way someone acts*
emancipated *to be free from the control or power of another*

expedition *a journey with a set purpose*
punishment *penalty inflicted on*

one after doing something wrong
social rank *a person's place and importance in society*

SLAVERY

This image from the Codex Vaticanus shows Chalchiuhtlicue, goddess of lakes and rivers, being attended by slaves.

No Aztecs were born into slavery, but they could become slaves for reasons that ranged from not paying tribute to losing bets. Criminals were made the slaves of those they had committed a crime against. Aztecs could also sell their children or themselves into slavery. In Aztec society, slaves were often given as a tribute payment by conquered tribes. The *Book of the Gods and Rites* shows male and female traders buying and selling slaves at a market. The slaves are shown wearing wooden collars around their necks to prevent escape. A slave might be able, however, to purchase his freedom at any time. Women who were slaves could also be freed by marrying their owners.

Source: Diego Durán, "The Book of the Gods and Rites and the Ancient Calendar," sixteenth century

Glossary

calpulli (singular: calpolli) large Aztec clans having their own leaders, temples, and schools, and who lived together in organized neighborhoods

clans groups connected by family ties or common interests or traits

economic related to the production, trade, and use of goods and services

livelihood way that one earns money or supports oneself

merchants people who trade for a living

pochteca Nahuatl word for merchants

social codes the rules that people in a society are expected to follow

society the people in a country and how they are organized

CASE STUDY

This stone model, found in the Great Temple, is of a pochteca using a headstrap to carry goods.

Traders

Merchants known as **pochteca** belonged to a special class of Aztec society. In the *Florentine Codex*, Spanish priest Bernardino de Sahagún shows three pictures of pochteca — seated before the emperor, traveling across Mexico, and trading jewelry and obsidian blades. Merchants were not allowed to display their wealth in public and returned to the capital at night, as Sahagún describes here:

*Not by day but by night they swiftly entered by boat ... And when he had quickly come to unload what he had acquired, then swiftly he took away his boat. When it dawned, nothing remained. ***

*Source: Bernardino de Sahagún, "Florentine Codex,"1580

See also: Language and Writing 10-11, Homes 12-13, Rulers 14-15, Growing Up Aztec 18-19

RELIGION AND SACRIFICE

The Aztecs worshiped more than two hundred gods. Every town, tribe, craft, and **social class** had its own god. The people also worshiped gods of creation, of rain and the different crops, and of war and death. The Aztecs were constantly trying to repay the gods by acts of sacrifice, in the hope that they might look kindly upon them.

AZTEC GODS

The Aztecs had gods of wind, fire, water, childbirth, disease, and misfortune, as well as gods of the sun, moon, and stars.

The sun god Huitzilopochtli, and the rain god Tlaloctwo were the two most important gods in the Aztec religion. Each was worshiped in his own **shrine** on the summit of the Great Temple. The Aztecs believed that the god **Quetzalcoatl** created humans:

*After the gods had assembled at Teotihuacan, and the sun had been created. they asked themselves who would inhabit the earth ... Quetzalcoatl approached Mictlantecuhtli and Mictlancihuatl (Lord and Lady of the region of the dead); at once he spoke to them: "I come in search of the precious bones in your possession." And Mictlantecuhtli asked of him "What shall you do with them, Quetzalcoatl?" once again Quetzalcoatl said "The gods are anxious that someone should inhabit the earth." ***

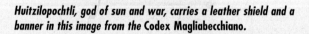

Huitzilopochtli, god of sun and war, carries a leather shield and a banner in this image from the Codex Magliabecchiano.

The Aztecs believed that after death a warrior who had been sacrificed or killed in battle went to the eastern paradise, women who died in childbirth went to the western paradise, people who had died by accident or disease went to the southern paradise of Tlaloc, and people who died of old age went to Mictlan, the land of the god of death Mictlantecuhtli.

*Source: Anonymous Mexican manuscript, 1558

Word Discovery

bloodthirsty *eager to kill or harm enough to shed blood*
deity *a god or goddess*
Omnipotent *all-powerful*

placate *calm or please someone by certain actions or words*
prayer *solemn request or thanks given to a god*

sacred *holy*
terrify *make someone feel very scared*

THE GREAT TEMPLE

This is the skull altar, or Tzompantli, at the Great Temple.

The Aztecs built a double temple called the *Templo Mayor*, or the Great Temple, for worshiping war god Huitzilopochtli and rain god Tlaloc. Partially excavated in 1978, the main temple courtyard originally covered almost 62 acres (25 hectares) and had seventy different buildings, including a **skull rack** for 136,000 human skulls, a ritual **ball court**, a stone for gladiator sacrifices, a temple to the god Xipe Totec for additional sacrifices, a temple to the god Quetzalcoatl, warriors' houses, and the priests' school. The scale of the Great Temple impressed all who saw it, including Hernán Cortés:

There are, in all districts of this great city, many temples or houses for their idols. Amongst these temples there is one, the principal one, whose great size and magnificence no human tongue can describe ...There are priests ... who live there permanently ... dress in black and never comb their hair.

Glossary

ball court the court on which the Aztec religious ball game *tlachtli* was played
Quetzalcoatl the priest god and god of learning and wind
ritual ceremony with set words or actions

shrine holy place for worshiping a god or a sacred person
skull rack a cage or box to hold the skulls of sacrificed humans
social class a person's rank in society

CASE STUDY

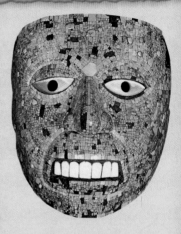

Turquoise mosaic mask worn while sacrificed to the god Quetzalcoatl.

Pyramid-temples and shrines at which the gods were worshiped through acts of **ritual** death have been found across the Aztec capital. The people practiced many forms of sacrifice. In a typical Aztec sacrifice, however, the victim was taken to the top of the Great Temple, stretched out on the sacrificial stone, his chest cut open, his heart ripped out, and his body thrown down the steps, as described here:

The usual method of sacrifice was to open the victim's chest, pull out his heart while he was still half-alive, and then knock down the man, rolling him down the temple steps which were awash with blood ... Six sacrificers came in ... four to hold the victim's feet and hands, another for the throat, and one to cut the chest and extract the victim's heart. They were called chachalmua, which in our language is the same thing as a minister of sacred things.[*]

*Source: José de Acosta, "Natural and Moral History of the Indies," 1590

See also: Origin of the Aztecs 4-5, Rise of an Empire 6-7, Aztec Time 20-21, Wars and Weapons 26-27

WARS AND WEAPONS

The Aztecs waged war in a different way than modern societies do today. Their wars were carried out in order to make enemies pay tribute and to capture prisoners for sacrifice to the gods. Victory meant gathering wealth in tribute payments from defeated enemies, not slaughtering thousands of people. The Aztecs did not have a **standing army**, but beginning at a young age, men were trained for battle. Boys were taught at school how to be warriors, and they were judged according to the number of prisoners they had captured in battle.

ELITE SOCIETIES

Archaeologists digging at the Great Temple site in Mexico City found two life-size, pottery statues guarding the entry to the main room.

Each statue represented a man dressed in the feathers of a giant eagle, with his head peering out of the bird's open beak. These statues matched illustrations from the codices of the Eagle Knights. The knights were members of one of the two great military societies that the best Aztec soldiers were invited to join. Another temple has been found at Malinalco, just outside Mexico City, dedicated to the two **elite** Aztec warrior societies of the Jaguar and the Eagle. European soldiers were amazed by the bravery of these Aztec soldiers and ranked them quite highly:

And I do not know how I can write this so calmly, because some three or four soldiers who were in Italy, who were there with us, swore many times to God, that they had never seen such ferocious fighting, like those that were found between Christians and against the artillery of the King of France, or of the Great Turk; nor men like those Indians, with so much courage in closing their ranks, and they said many other things, and the reasons they gave for them, as they would later see. *

This Eagle Warrior statue is one of two recovered from the Great Temple.

*Source: Bernal Diaz del Castillo, "The Conquest of New Spain," sixteenth century

Word Discovery

captive *taken and held as a prisoner*
discipline *bring under control through training and order*

fearsome *causing fear*
flamboyant *brightly colored and very fancy*

tactics *in war, the art of organizing and moving an army in battle*

WEAPONS

Aztec body armor was made out of strengthened cotton and was more for **show** than for genuine protection from injury on the battlefield. Warriors carried shields decorated with feathers and mosaic or gold and turquoise **inlay**. Their weapons ranged from javelins and bows to slings and swords. Javelins were launched with spear-throwers called *atlatl* that let warriors cover a greater distance with this weapon. Swords called *maquahuitl* were made of wood with edges of obsidian blades that would have been sharp enough to slice straight through an enemy's body.

Aztec warfare gear: feathered shield, made of gold and feathers, showing a coyote or ahuitzol, a mythical water creature (above); and a spear thrower (below)

CASE STUDY

In the Codex Mendoza, an Aztec warrior is shown capturing an enemy soldier by grasping his hair.

War of Flowers

Flower Wars, called *xochiyaoyotl*, were designed to capture prisoners for sacrifice to the gods, rather than to win territory. This was a special type of warfare. Priests observed the battles and ended the **hostilities** once they decided enough prisoners had been taken. The name *Flower Wars* refers to the costumes of warriors and how they fell in battle like a shower of blossoms. The brother of Moctezuma I urged young men to join these wars:

*Huitzilopochtli, the young warrior who acts above! He follows my path! Not in vain did I dress myself in yellow plumes, for I am he who has caused the sun to rise.**

Glossary

atlatl a device used for throwing javelins farther than normal
elite superior
hostilities acts of warfare or fighting
inlay set into another material

maquahuitl a sword-club, with an obsidian cutting-edge
show outward appearance
standing army a permanent, professional army

*Source: Miguel León-Portilla "Aztec Thought and Culture," sixteenth century

See also: Rise of an Empire 6-7, Rulers 14-15, Growing Up Aztec 18-19, Religion and Sacrifice 24-25

LEISURE

Having fun was very important in the Aztec empire. The Aztec people loved hunting, gambling, and games, such as **tlachtli** and **patolli**. Many of these games had underlying religious meanings and were taken very seriously, sometimes ending in death or **destitution** for the loser. Music, poetry, and dance were also important activities, and children learned at an early age how to dance properly. The Aztecs used these skills in the many religious festivals they celebrated each year.

GAMES

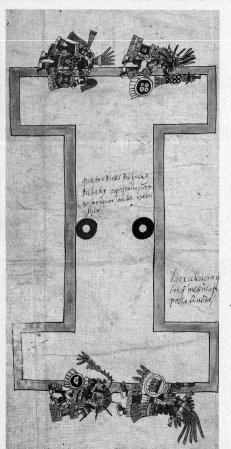

Tlachtli was a ball game played only by nobles. It was played on a large court shaped like the letter *I*. The goal was for players to put the ball through one of two vertical hoops on the sides of the court using just their knees and hips. The court represented the world, while the ball stood for the Sun or Moon. People often placed bets on the game. In a match he played against the lord of Xochimilco, Emperor Axayacatl bet the Great Marketplace. Rather than accept his defeat graciously, Axayacatl had his soldiers kill his opponent:

*While they saluted him and made him presents, they threw a garland of flowers about his neck with a **thong** hidden in it, and so killed him.**

Patolli was a gambling, board game played with dice. Like tlachtli, it had a religious meaning. The board had fifty-two squares, the number of years in the dual calendar, and Aztecs believed that the god **Macuilxochitl** watched over every game.

Ball game, from Codex Borbonicus, a sixteenth-century, post-conquest manuscript

*Source: "Codex Ixtlilxochitl," sixteenth century

Word Discovery

destiny *fate or something meant to happen*
leisure *time away from work*
that is spent as one wants
retribution *something inflicted as a punishment*
victor *someone who defeats an enemy or opponent*

MUSIC, SINGING, AND DANCING

The Aztecs loved music, singing, and dancing. The main instruments in an Aztec band were the drums, which provided the beat to which the people **chanted**. Other instruments included hollow shells, pottery whistles, and rattles, so apart from the singing, Aztec music did not have much **melody**. The dances and music played at religious festivals was often highly ritualized and needed to be absolutely perfect. If a musician or singer spoiled a song at the court of Moctezuma, the performer was put to death. Spanish observers were intrigued by Aztec music but found the dancing offensive:

Young people took great pride in their ability to dance, sing, and guide the others in the dances ... There was another dance so roguish ... with all its wriggling and grimacing and immodest mimicry ... it is highly improper. *

An Aztec dance, from Diego Durán's 1579 manuscript Historia de las Indias

*Source: Diego Durán, "The History of the Indies of New Spain," sixteenth century

Glossary

chanted sang repeated phrases
destitution loss of all money and property
Macuilxochitl Five Flowers, the Aztec god of music and dance
melody pleasant arrangement of sounds

patolli a gambling, board game
philosopher teacher or student of wisdom
thong a leather whip
tlachtli ball game played by teams on a special court

See also: Language and Writing 10-11, Rulers 14-15, Growing Up Aztec 18-19

CASE STUDY

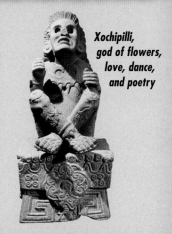

Xochipilli, god of flowers, love, dance, and poetry

Aztec Poetry

Art, literature, and poetry were an important part of Aztec life. Priests and nobles prided themselves on their skill in these arts, while some emperors were also renowned for their poetry. The Aztec word for poetry means "flowers and song." The concept of flowers reoccurs throughout their poems as a symbol of beauty, life, and the gods. An Aztec writer believed that his poems were one way he could live forever. Aztec poetry reflects the people's worry about what happens after death. This poem from the **philosopher** king Nezahualcoyotl of Texcoco (1403–1473) expresses his concern:

One day we must go, one night we will descend into the region of mystery. Here, we only come to know ourselves; only in passing are we here on earth ... Would that one lived forever; would that one were not to die. *

*Source: Diego Durán, "The History of the Indies of New Spain," sixteenth century

THE END OF THE AZTECS

By 1517, Spaniards exploring the coast of Mexico were returning with stories of a fabulous city situated high in the mountains. Hernán Cortés persuaded the governor of Cuba to let him make an expedition to find this city. Cortés gathered together a fleet of ships, soldiers, sailors, crossbowmen, and **musketeers**, and on November 8, 1519, he and his **conquistadors** marched into Tenochtitlán to meet Moctezuma II. Just a few years later, they would completely destroy the Aztec empire.

SPANISH INVASION

When the Spanish arrived in Mexico, they were greeted with awe by the Aztecs, who viewed the white, bearded beings in metal armor as gods.

Even Aztec emperor Moctezuma II trusted the Spanish completely and gave Cortés a warm welcome, as described here:

Moctezuma, the great and powerful prince of Mexico ... sent five chieftains of the highest ranks to our camp ... to bid us welcome ... When we entered the town (of Tlaxcala) there was no room in the streets or on the roofs, so many men and women having come out with happy faces to see us.*

The Spanish reported that the mood soon changed once Cortés revealed his **intentions**:

*On entering the palace, Cortés made his usual **salutations**, and said to Moctezuma: "If you cry out, or raise any commotion, you will immediately be killed by these captains of mine, whom I have brought for this sole purpose."**

In this painting from the Tlaxcala walls, Hernán Cortés is shown meeting the Aztecs.

*Source: Bernal Diaz del Castillo, "The Conquest of New Spain," sixteenth century

Word Discovery

contagious spread by direct or indirect contact

disease an illness that affects a main function of the body

dismantle take apart into small pieces

overwhelm overpower

revolution overthrow of one ruler or government for another

FALL OF TENOCHTITLÁN

Sixteenth-century illustration of the Battle for Tenochtitlán

After they arrived in Tenochtitlán, the Spanish troops stayed in the city. While there, Spanish forces **massacred** thousands of members of the Aztec nobility, creating an uproar. Moctezuma II was even taken **hostage** for a time. Later, he tried to calm a restless Aztec crowd but was killed by a stone thrown at him. Eventually, Aztec forces surrounded the palaces where the Spanish were living and forced them out, inflicting heavy losses. In 1521, Hernán Cortés returned to Tenochtitlán with seven hundred Spanish soldiers and seventy thousand native troops, including the Tlaxcalan army. He **besieged** the city until, in August 1521, it surrendered. The Spaniards and their **allies** entered the city and massacred the people. The last Aztec ruler, Cuauhtemoc, was captured and hanged. Writer Fernando de Alva Ixtlilxochitl recorded the tragic scene:

Almost all those Aztec nobility died, the only survivors being a few lords and gentlemen, mostly children or extremely young people.*

*Source: Fernando de Alva Ixtlilxochitl, "Historia de la Nación Chichemeca," sixteenth century

Glossary

allies two or more groups with common goals or interests

besieged surrounded a place with an army until those inside surrendered

conquistadors Spanish word for conquerors; leaders in Spanish army

hostage a prisoner held until something is given up or paid

intentions what one plans to do

massacred killed many people brutally, usually those unable to fight back

musketeers soldiers who fought with a musket — an early form of rifle

salutations greetings

CASE STUDY

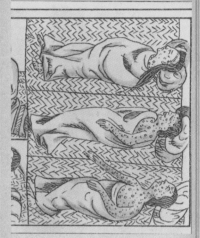

This illustration of Aztec women suffering from smallpox is taken from the Florentine Codex.

Smallpox

Cortés conquered the Aztec empire. The man who did the most to destroy it, however, was an unnamed Spanish soldier who came to help Cortés in April 1520 — and who had smallpox. The Aztecs had no immunity to this new disease and over the next two years perhaps half a million of them died from it. A tiny germ proved to be a more powerful weapon than all of Cortés' guns and horses. Bernal Diaz describes the spread of the disease:

The disease spread with inconceivable rapidity, and the Indians died by thousands; for not knowing the nature of it they brought it to a fatal issue by throwing themselves into cold water in the heat of the disorder.*

*Source: Bernal Díaz del Castillo, "The Conquest of New Spain," sixteenth century

See also: Rulers 14-15, Aztec Society 22-23, Religion and Sacrifice 24-25, Wars and Weapons 26-27

Index

AZTEC TIME LINE

1175
Fall of Toltec civilization

1200
Arrival of Aztecs in Central Mexico

1250
Aztecs move to Valley of Mexico

1325
Tenochtitlán built

1372
First Aztec tlatoani appointed

1426
Escalation of conflict between Aztecs and Tepanecs

1428
Aztec empire established with victory of the Triple Alliance

1519–1521
Spanish conquest

1520
Last Aztec emperor appointed

PICTURE CREDITS: Art Archive: Title, 4, 5br, 6, 7tr, 8, 9 (both), 10, 11br, 12, 14, 16, 17 (both), 18, 19tr, 20, 21 (both), 22, 23 (both), 24, 25tl, 27tr, 28l, 28-29c, 29tr, 30, 31 (both); **Corbis** 7l; **Michael Smith:** 13 (both); **Werner Forman Archive:** 11t, 15 (both), 19tl, 25tr, 26, 27tl, 27cl.